W9-BYF-721

COOL CAREERS in VIDEO GAMES

SCHOLASTIC

New York • Toronto • London • Auckland • Sydney
Mexico City • New Delhi • Hong Kong

ISBN 978-0-545-81916-9

Previously published as *Hot Jobs in Video Games*.

10 9 8 7   16 17 18 19/0

Printed in the U.S.A. 40
This edition first printing, January 2015

Written by Joe Funk
with Dean Takahashi

Writing and Design by: www.Mojo-Media.com
Contributing Editor: Trevor Talley
Creative Director: Jason Hinman

To my children, Joey and Janey, and kids everywhere—may they reach for and realize their dreams with courage and courtesy.

Thanks to everyone who made this book, a most worthy cause, possible. Any mistakes are solely mine.

table of contents

8   Making a Game

10 Video Games Evangelist

20 We Can Be Heroes

24 Animation Station

34 From Digital Artist to Chief Executive

44 Going Great Guns

54 Art Simulates Life

62 Calling the Game

72 Paid to Play

76 Imagining Mayhem

86 Writing for Fun & Games

90 Job Glossary

introduction

ave you ever found yourself playing one of your favorite video games and wondered what it was like to make one? Did you ever find yourself immersed in an environment so cool that you thought about it long after you were done playing?

Welcome to the dominant mediums of the twenty-first century: video games and interactive entertainment!

Whether you like *Mario*, *Madden*, or *Master Chief*, or *Minecraft*, or getting wild with a Wii, there's no doubt that video games are fun to play, and if you're a creative person who likes using a computer, you may want to consider video games for a career.

Getting a gig in the video games industry does not have to be just a dream; it requires the same skills that you're learning in school every day, including art, reading, writing, math, and computers.

This book will give you a better understanding of what it takes to create a video game, and highlight a few of the many jobs you can get in the industry. From legendary game creators to people who actually make a living playing video games, this book will give you an insightful introduction to this fascinating and fast-evolving medium.

Making A Game

How it's done:
The video game production process

The production of a video game, going from a simple idea to a finished product on store shelves, is a challenging but rewarding process that can take years. Along the way, many different people and teams develop the project in a progression of stages.

IDEA Usually it all begins when a producer, an executive, a designer, or an artist—good ideas can spring from anyone—comes up with a new game concept or idea and becomes the **champion** of the idea. This initial spark may be a basic story line, scenario, experience, or perhaps a sequel, enhancement, or spin-off of a previous game.

CONCEPT TESTING The champion usually then comes up with a **game pitch document**. The game pitch document outlines the basics of the game along with a few of its unique selling points or features. Depending on the developer, a small team led by the champion is asked to do a prototype for demonstration to see if the concept is viable, or a concept testing company is hired to test and evaluate the game idea. Concept testing, or prototyping, usually happens before any sort of script or backstory, plots, etc., are made, because if the core concept or prototype isn't fun, there's not much sense in developing it further.

GAME DESIGN DOCUMENT Once a game concept is approved, a **game design document (GDD)**, which includes concept sketches of game characters, levels, enemies, and more, is created. The GDD becomes the bible that will be used to bring the game to life.

CREATIVE DEVELOPMENT Three-dimensional designs of all the game's characters, items, enemies, and environments are generated on computers so the design team can figure out how they want them to move and act. Typically, concept artists flesh out a character based on collaboration between the artists and designers. Three-dimensional (3-D) modelers then use computers to create the character based on the concept art.

ANIMATION The art team focuses on specifics like facial features and expressions while a character is speaking— tiny details that take a ton of work to get right. Specialized artists, called animators, either capture and polish **motion capture** or hand-animate frames not easily motion captured by using a more intensive process called **key framing**. Developers then gather and generate a pile of data about the finer points of each character in the game. Research has to be done on historical games to make sure outfits are correct. Designers will observe athletes, soldiers, or vehicles in motion and attempt to create characters that mimic these actions as accurately as possible.

AUDIO After a script is written and approved, sound effects are compiled and voice actors are hired to create each character—and all of it is digitally recorded for use in the game's programming. Audio specialists also record (or create) sound effects as needed for the game, such as the cheering of a crowd, the growling of animals, the chirping of birds, or the sounds of various guns firing.

PROGRAMMING While developing a cohesive story line and distinctive art is the first step in the game development process, programming code—that is, creating the software instructions to re-create the game on your computer—is perhaps the most difficult and time-consuming step. Programmers need to have a firm grasp of multiple computer programming languages, as well as an understanding of computer logic and mathematics. A base of code, called the **game engine**, is compiled from scratch or tweaked from a previous game to give the programmers a basic toolbox for their specific assignments. Programmers may have hundreds of tasks that can take anywhere from half a day to a few weeks to complete and debug. Some games take three to four years to create! Programmers create 3-D designs of all the backgrounds, cut scenes, characters, level designs, and sound effects, with the goal of combining them into one coherent game experience. This involves a massive, coordinated team effort, as well as the patience to deal with the grind that comes from long hours and painstaking details.

PLAY TESTING When the programming team nears completion of its task and all of the code and content is assembled, the game is tested. There are typically a lot of art, design, and code bugs to iron out at this stage, so playability testers, focus testers, and designers play the game inside and out, looking for any bugs, errors, or glitches. They play the same portions of the game over and over, sometimes for months, looking for the smallest bugs that need to be fixed, then pass along their findings to the programming team for correction. Playability testers are also responsible for giving their opinion of the game, such as whether the control scheme is easy to use and whether the game has the appropriate feel that the designers were aiming for. Once everything noted by the testers is addressed by the programmers, the game is approved by the team leaders and goes into production. (On rare occasions, if the problems are deemed not fixable, a project is canceled.)

PRODUCTION As a game nears completion, a firm release date is set, giving the production staff a final deadline. At this point the marketing and sales teams kick into high gear, hyping the game to retailers, the media, and the public. The game's final code is compiled and burned to a single master disc, which is then used to mass-produce copies of the game. The game disc is inserted into that familiar plastic packaging and is ready for shipping to retailers.

In 2011, Lutz helped launch *Call of Duty: Modern Warfare 3* by hosting a live fan celebration and million-dollar gaming event.

video games evangelist

Monte Lutz
Global Head of PR, Activision

How do you hear about video games? Think for a second about the last game you played. When did you go from never having heard of it to knowing it existed?

Chances are you heard about it in one of two ways: Either a friend told you about it, or you saw an advertisement for it. As one of the world's fastest growing industries, video-game advertisements come in all sorts of formats, from TV spots to billboards to little blinking banner ads on web pages and more. These ads are full of images and information that excite people and get them talking.

But do you know where those ads come from? Each one of these ads is very carefully and thoughtfully crafted by people like

Monte Lutz, who work in a special branch of work called public relations, or P.R.

Mr. Lutz runs the P.R. department of Activision Publishing Inc., the first independent distributor and publisher of games for consoles starting with the Atari 2600. If you're a gamer, it's pretty likely that you've spent at least a few hours with an Activision game, which include classics like *Pitfall!* and *Tony Hawk's Pro Skater,* as well as more contemporary games such as *Guitar Hero, Skylanders* and *Destiny.*

As the Global Head of Public Relations at Activision, Monte Lutz is deeply involved with disseminating information about Activision's newest titles to the world. Activision describes this as, "telling the stories of some of the most popular entertainment franchises on the planet." In order to tell those stories, Lutz and his team of P.R. experts think creatively about how to let fans know when new games are to hit stores and what players can expect from those games.

Activision's P.R. strategies for games take many forms. According to Lutz, "Not only do we work with traditional media and bloggers, we partner with more than 100 YouTubers who love playing our games. It's a global team and an amazing group. P.R. is integrated deeply with the digital, events and marketing teams. It's one organization, with the singular mission of getting people excited about playing awesome games. Plus, I get the chance to play them a year before they come out. Not a bad job indeed."

Of course, public relations is not typically the first thing that comes to mind when people think about gaming jobs. Even Lutz's seven-year-old daughter has it slightly wrong: "She tells her friends that I 'make' *Skylanders*," said Lutz. "That sounds like the coolest job in the world to a seven-year-old." However, Lutz's job is is also immensely important. His role is to skillfully handle the release of a game, so people around the world know about it. "Well, I don't quite make *Skylanders*. But I do get to introduce *Skylanders* to the world and decide which parts of the *Skylanders* story are told first."

Lutz's career path was unique as well. "When I graduated from college, I moved from California to Colorado to work at the national headquarters of Junior Achievement, an educational non-profit. It was a P.R. job, but with the opportunity to evolve the company's early digital strategy. [Junior Achievement] gave me the chance to work on my first Super Bowl ad, the famous 'When I Grow Up' ad with Monster.com, and to open an exhibit

One of Monte Lutz's most recent projects was working on the P.R. for *Destiny*, a game that went on to have one of the most successful entertainment title releases in history in September 2014.

at Chicago's Museum of Science and Industry, which was my favorite museum from when I was a kid."

From there, Lutz followed a passion for politics to Washington D.C., where he said he "produced town hall events for members of Congress" and "went on to become a speechwriter, and to develop marketing campaigns for government agencies, including NASA, USDA, and the Departments of Labor and Education."

Never one to rest on past accomplishments, Lutz has since worked on dozens of interesting projects that run the gamut of the P.R. world and beyond, including launching a magazine, writing a book (*Social Pulpit*, which teaches social-media tactics based on Barack Obama's successful run for the presidency), teaching at Johns Hopkins University, joining the world's biggest

P.R. agency (Edelman) and working on brands such as the NFL, the MLB, MTV, Volkswagen, Microsoft, StubHub, PayPal, Starz, and more.

Eventually, he said, "I got the call from Activision. *Call of Duty: Modern Warfare 3* was about to launch, and Activision was hosting Call of Duty XP, a chance for 7,000 fans to celebrate the game through paintball matches in recreated *Call of Duty* levels, zip lines courses, off-road Jeep adventures, an opportunity to play the upcoming game, and a million-dollar *Call of Duty* tournament. They were looking for help in engaging with fans through social media."

Games were something Lutz had always loved, starting with Activision's own 1982 title *Pitfall!* "When I was a kid, I used to play *Pitfall!* with my sister," he said. "She was wicked good, and used to take Polaroid pictures and send them in for badges from

the game." He was also a huge fan of arcade games. "*Defender, Donkey Kong, Pac-Man,* and *Frogger*—all the classics," he said. He once played a black-and-white watch-based version of *Q-bert* the entire way from Houston to Chicago (1,083 miles), which cemented his passion for games at an early age.

Years later, Lutz "jumped at the chance" to join Activision, the company whose games he grew up with. "Almost 30 years later, life has come full circle," he said. "I work for Activision, the company that made *Pitfall!* all those years ago. Now I have more badges than I could ever hope for."

After working for so many different organizations, Lutz decided that Activision and gaming were where he wanted to put his talent and experience. "My mind and my time kept on drifting back to Activision," he said. "I helped create the social-media campaigns for the launch of *Call of Duty: Black Ops II,*

Skylanders Giants, and other games. But it was only part of my day. In September 2013, I made the jump to Activision full time, to become the Global Head of P.R. It was baptism by fire hose from day one: launching *Skylanders SWAP Force* and *Call of Duty: Ghosts* within 60 days of joining the company. A year later, I've helped to evolve how we think about P.R. and how we connect with fans."

Considering how successful Activision's titles have been in the last few years, it's safe to say that Lutz knows what he's doing when it comes to connecting with fans. Lutz's career is a great example of what one can do within the gaming industry, aside from coding and designing.

Lutz offers the following advice to young gamers and, perhaps, some future P.R. superstars interested in the gaming industry:

"When we are small kids, we read the same book a hundred times and watch the same TV show a dozen times or more, because it's awesome and we love it. We play the same level of a game and enjoy it every time. Nobody is there to tell us that we can't experience that one thing over and over and over again, or that we should move on to the next big thing. When we get a bit older, people think that if they're not constantly moving forward and doing something different, they'll be instantly bored. We always have to have something new, new, new, forgetting that some of the best things in life are the ones you've always loved.

"By the time you are an adult, you can simplify things again and choose what you live simply for the love of it. When your favorite movie comes on TV, you watch it for the hundredth time, even though it's too late and you should really just fall asleep instead. When you pick up your favorite book, you take the time to read the notes in the margins and realize that you were a completely different person the last time you read it. You don't have to do everything, be everything, consume everything. You don't have to always move on to the next thing. You pick what you love and throw yourself into it completely again.

"Whether it's the games you choose to play, the subjects you study in school, or the career you choose when you finish school, make the choice based on what you would choose to do every day if you could only choose to do one thing." ■

WE CAN BE HEROES

Randy Ma
DC COMICS

Job Skills Needed: Reading; Research; Communication

Batman and his super-hero friends are big deals, leaping out of the comic pages where they originated to places far beyond. The denizens of the DC Comics universe are known and loved all over the world through a variety of media. In fact, the Batman movie franchise is ranked among the top 10 in the world as far as money is concerned, right up there with Harry Potter and Star Wars.

As part of the extremely successful DC universe, there are, of course, more than a few video games. Super-hero stories are ideal for gaming, with their iconic good guys, dynamic bad guys, and feats of super-human power. This is the stuff of good storytelling and great gaming!

Creating a game is a monumental task that requires dozens of experts in technical fields, but there are other jobs every bit as

important as the programmers and animators. Randy Ma has such a job. He is the Creative Associate for Interactive at DC Entertainment. Ma is responsible for knowing just about everything in the DC Comics universe and making sure every character in a game is properly represented and true to form. "If Batman is used in a kid's game or a teen game," said Ma, "[it's important] he still remains the caped crusader we love and recognize. He is a defender of justice with strong morals and a distaste for guns."

Ma describes his work in this way: "My job responsibilities include testing all DC video games, reviewing game design pitches, artwork, story scripts, and a lot of research. It is my job to know the entirety of DC Comics from its characters and history. If a game developer has an idea, it is my responsibility to foster the creativity and help guide their vision so it fits with the

DC universe. I will offer my expertise for possible super heroes, villains, and locations for their game, but also provide them with actual comic books to read to help inspire them on how they would like to interpret our characters."

One of the challenges of Ma's job is to find the balance between keeping the game true to the DC universe and letting the game creators do their jobs by being creative. "As important as it is to make sure Superman's powers are correctly used and shown in the game, it is also very important not to hinder the creativity of our game developers," he said. "It is a collaborative process where the goal is not only to make the best possible DC game, but also a fun game for the players."

Like many in the gaming world, Ma's path to his current job was indirect. He originally worked in movies, but spent his free time working on a video-gaming blog where he analyzed games. Later, he worked as a tester at Activision and then as an intern with rival company Marvel. His experience in the worlds of comics and gaming positioned Ma for his current role, as did a growing desire to be more involved in game development.

When asked for advice to kids looking to get into the video-game industry, Ma said he wished he had taken more time when he was younger to learn the technical aspects of the game, such as programming. While it hasn't hampered his success, he said it would have helped him later on.

It's never too early to start thinking about your future in games, he said. Even little things can help you in big ways later on. "If you enjoy playing games and are thinking about a career in the industry, start identifying what it is about the games you like," he said. "What kind of games do you like to play and why? What kind of game would you like to make for others to play? Make simple games using pen and paper, and get some friends together to play. Or come up with ways to make games you play already more fun, even simple games like tic-tac-toe or football. And if you are so bold as to want to make your own video game, there are plenty of resources online—from YouTube to message boards and websites—to help get you started."

So next time you take control of a digital Batman and swing a punch at a baddie, remember there' a man named Randy Ma who made sure that he's swinging just as he would in the comics. ■

Animation Stations

Kat Curry
Character Animator, Disney Online Studios
The World of Cars Online

Job Skills Needed: Drawing; Anatomy; Computers

Kat is a character animator for Disney/Pixar's *The World of Cars Online*. Her job is to make characters come to life by creating performances that seem physically and emotionally believable and entertaining. "I don't make explosions or buildings fall apart," she says, laughing. "That's for the visual effects animators."

With her fascination for the stop-motion creature movies created by Ray Harryhausen, including *Jason and the Argonauts* and *The Beast from 20,000 Fathoms*, it struck Kat that stop-motion animation wasn't so different from playing with her toys in the backyard when she was a kid, bending their arms and legs to make them look like they were walking or acting out scenes. Kat also loved the behind-the-scenes peeks on *The Wonderful*

24

fast fact

The first Pixar production to not feature a human being, *Cars*—in both movie and video game form—presented a unique challenge for character animators to create emotion.

fast fact

The World of Cars Online is a kid-safe, virtual world based on the animated feature *Cars*. In the game, kids can design their own car characters and they interact with all of their favorite cast members.

World of Disney every Sunday night. "It was something I looked forward to," she recalls. "They often showed animators at work, and how the movies were made, and I just knew I always wanted to do that."

Her career arc, like many, was not a straightforward path. After attending a four-year college and earning a degree in math, Kat spent many years as a computer graphics programmer and took art classes on the side. She briefly went to a visual effects school where she focused on character-related topics such as rigging, hair and cloth simulation, and animation. It was there, she says, that she "realized [her] true love was animation and not so much the technology part."

While at the effects school, she got her first opportunity working on a Disney project as a character rigger. Riggers (in CGI) make movable skeletons for character models and provide controls for the animator to use. After that, she worked mostly in movies, sometimes doing crowd simulation, rigging, or

Racing at the Carburetor Country Speedway in The World of Cars Online.

animation. "I took every opportunity to do character animation when it was available, but was glad I had other background skills when it wasn't," she recalls. "And no, you certainly don't need a math degree or [to] know how to program to be an animator. I'm glad I did those things, but there are many different paths to becoming an animator."

She reminds kids that there are many options just in animation alone, so it helps to know what you like. "Not all animation jobs are the same, and some are more technical than others," she says. There is a big difference between traditional cartoon animation and motion capture, which is when multiple sensors are placed on

(above) Exploring Red Hood Valley in *The World of Cars Online*. (opposite) Customizing your car in your garage.

In *The World of Cars Online*, you can trick out and customize your car in a number of ways, and then work your way up from dirt track racing to competing for the Piston Cup.

someone like an athlete or soldier to sense motion that is then translated to the on-screen character to animate him or her in a very fluid and lifelike way. "A large percentage of games involve motion capture," she says. "Sometimes you need to do very realistic work, and sometimes very cartoony. It is good to know which you prefer, so it's good to experiment with a lot of different styles and media, including stop-motion, traditional, and flash."

As animation evolves from ink and paper to the computer screen, Kat says the creativity must still come from within. "Technology has made it possible to create any visual image you want. So the real challenge is coming up with a good idea

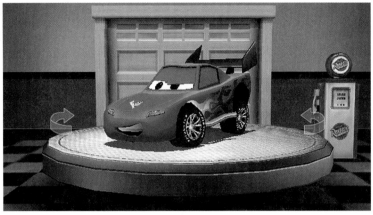

and a great performance. Many people can animate, but not everyone can create a really cool character. The job market is incredibly competitive and globalized. You need to be a dedicated artist to be doing this for a living. Simply learning a piece of software will not make your career."

Despite the necessity of learning computers, Kat believes that a well-rounded lifestyle and the ability to observe the world around oneself are important pillars of success as well. "Step away from the computer," she advises. "Find other stuff to do in the real world. Not only will you have fun, but it will make you a better animator. And you'll have better stories to tell if you go out into the world and have adventures. Take acting or dance, and take art classes. Develop your own sense of style. Take note of funny or weird things that happen in your life, even if you're waiting in line at the grocery store just observing what other people are doing. You never know where you will find your next great idea."

Fillmore's Fields in *The World of Cars Online.*

One of her favorite things to do outside of her job is play sports, such as Ultimate Frisbee. "It gives me a natural sense of weight and timing, confidence, and knowing how to work with a team of people. These things are as critical to being a great animator as anything else."

As for aspiring animators out there, Kat has some words of wisdom: "People in this field come in all shapes and sizes and ages. You may have heard stereotypes about animators being all crazy and extroverted, but that's not the case. Some are quiet and some are nutty. Be who you are and develop your personal interests. It will make your animation more interesting for people to watch." ■

TOW MATER ANIMATION SEQUENCE

From Digital Artist to Chief Executive

Louis Castle
Game Designer, Co-Founder
Westwood Studios

Job Skills: Forward Thinking; Eye for Aesthetics; Boldness; Knowledge of the Fie

Some people become game designers because that's what they've always wanted to do, but this is not always the case. Many designers, in fact many *legendary* designers, found themselves making games after following a different passion, which over the years led them to the world of video game creation.

One such designer and, indeed, legend of the video gaming community who found his way to games through outside interests is Louis Castle. Co-founder of the famed Westwood Studios, Castle is a man who has held an enormous number of important positions at a variety of games companies, including EA, GarageGames, and Zynga. Though Castle was a born gamer ("I had always enjoyed board games and role playing games."), it was actually a passion for digital art that led to his helping to create one of the most successful video game studios of the 90s

and, eventually, a long and storied career in gaming.

As a visual artist, Castle found computers fascinating as a conduit for expression. As he says, "I was drawn into game development in the early 80s, as I looked for a way to use computers as an art medium. Originally I bought a computer to learn CAD for a career in architecture, but was struck by how vibrant the color was on the screen. I was exploring Rothko's work and thought that in the future, galleries would hang monitors in addition to canvases."

Castle was eager to see what he could make computers do to create art, and this interest manifested itself in a focus on the new field of imagery animated by computers. "I was also interested in animation, but was frustrated by the poor performance of the early micro-computers. This was before the days of graphics

Red Alert 2 (seen above) was the 7th full installment in the *Command & Conquer* series of games, which as of 2014 has over 20 full titles and expansions under its banner.

editing tools, so I learned low-level programming to both control how my artwork was presented and to push for better animation performance. Games were the perfect vehicle to work on both images and animations."

While in college for a combination of a Master of Fine Arts degree and a Computer Science degree, Louis met Brett Sperry, and together the two started working as contractors for various computer gaming developers. According to Castle, "Our first break was signing an agreement with Epyx Games in March of 1985 to port Jon Freemen's *Temple of Apshai* Trilogy of games from the Commodore 64 to the Macintosh. This allowed the birth of Westwood Studios." This, as he says, allowed Castle and Sperry

the ability "to work directly with publishers."

With the combined skills of Sperry and Castle ("I was the low-level programmer and artist, while Brett focused on design and business."), Westwood began putting out games that had solid central concepts and a very distinct aesthetic sense about them, in addition to being just plain fun to play. Armed with the artistic sensibilities of Castle and Sperry's business acumen, it didn't take long for the industry to take notice of what Westwood was doing: "Our first major original success was 5 years (after founding Westwood) when we created *Eye of the Beholder*, a dungeon crawling RPG with the Dungeons and Dragon's license, for Strategic Simulations, Inc. I would (also) be remiss not to mention *Dune II,* which was the first RTS game; followed by *Command & Conquer,* which propelled our company from a boutique developer to international industry leader."

Indeed, Westwood's *Dune II* and *Command & Conquer*

Louis Castle and his fellows at Westwood brought something new into the gaming market with *Dune II,* a game based on the famous book series and which was the title that would come to define the Real Time Stragegy genre.

outright changed the gaming scene by introducing an entirely new genre that still thrives today in the Real Time Strategy game (RTS), without which such games as *League of Legends* and *DOTA 2* would not exist. The continued success of Westwood not only allowed the studio to expand its scope and scale enormously, eventually leading to their acquisition by Virgin Games in 1992, it also gave Castle a space to grow as a developer. "As Westwood grew, I took on more leadership and director roles, eventually adding design and production to my daily craft work," he says, and after many years as a designer, he "moved into the role of COO and CFO as we grew from 29 workers to over two hundred."

In 1998, the stories of Westwood and Castle's career took

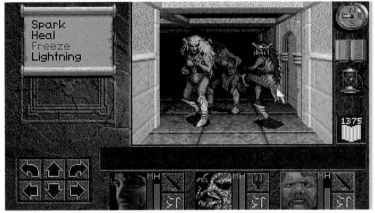

another mighty leap forward, as the gaming behemoth EA purchased the company, giving Castle access to even more tools and resources to create his vision of video gaming. "While at EA," he says, "I worked on even larger senior leadership roles; but also started some new studio initiatives with small teams, resulting in a good deal of hands on work."

Starting from an interest in video games as an artist medium (that now seems a humble beginning for the man), Castle's extensive and field-spanning work at Westwood and then EA has led to a point where he is now able to essentially choose where he wants to work and what he wants to work on. In the last few years this has driven him to jump back into the world of smaller studios like Zynga: "In my most recent roles, I was able to influence many parts of many projects, so I was always excited to get to work on the next challenge. I found I missed the hands-on nature of being with a small team and building a game, so recently I have been contracting with smaller companies in order

Westwood Studios has never been one to hide from innovation, and they've put out critical hits in many genres. 1997's *Blade Runner,* for example, was the first game to run its world as fully 3-D rendered and in real time, and it was named PC Gamer's "Best Adventure Game of 1997."

to have a direct influence on games before going back into a bigger leadership role."

As someone who has not only "made it" in the gaming world, but who has influenced the very direction that world has taken, Castle looks back at his success with an interesting and informed perspective. We asked him what he wished he'd known starting out that he does now, and he gave us the following, somewhat tongue-in-cheek gem: "To buy Apple stock. In all seriousness, I think it was the not knowing what I know now that allowed many of my successes. Confidence and ignorance allowed me to presume I could do things that were statistically improbable. Not knowing how much work building a company would take allowed me to rush in with no fear. Tenacity and a desire to build the kind of place I wanted to work at every day propelled me to take risks

I would never advise at this point in my life."

Perhaps most remarkable about Castle, a man whose biography includes holding the titles of "Artist, Programmer, Art Director, Technical Director, Designer, Studio GM, COO, CFO, CCO, CSO, and CEO" and who has won not only many DICE Awards, but also a BAFTA and the second-ever Games Developers Conference Lifetime Achievement Award, is that he still loves his job and the industry that has allowed him to do such great work. "The best part about the games industry is that the big changes and opportunities are largely unpredictable. This allows small creative groups in the right place at the right time to completely disrupt the status quo."

And this passion and love for what video games can do is something Castle wants to share. When asked if he had any advice for kids who would like to make games themselves, Castle told us, "YOU are the best judge of what will be the next big thing. Take on a project you love; work hard; keep borrowing to the bare

minimum to avoid mortgaging your future. Find like-minded people with talents different than your own and follow your passion. It is easier to gain skills at an established company, but don't settle if you feel you don't belong. You may not be as lucky as I have been, but if you stay true to your internal compass, you will lead a happy and productive life in a career that is very rewarding. That's far better than settling for a job where you spend only a small portion of your waking hours doing what you love."

Considering that games are supposed to be fun, it only makes sense that a man who has made over 100 of them in his life thinks that making them should be fun too. And as an example for those who love games, but wonder if their skills would work in the gaming industry, Castle's career is perfect. Because, as he and so many others have said, "I just never imagined being able to make a living doing what I loved to do as hobbies." And yet, here he is; making great games all these years after turning what he loves into an iconic career. ∎

Going Great Guns

Cliff Bleszinski
Creator and Design Director, Epic Games
Unreal; Gears of War

Job Skills Needed: Creativity; Computers; Management

Gamers around the world know the work of Cliff, the creator of Microsoft and Epic Games' bestselling *Gears of War* franchise. In addition to the blockbuster video games, toys, novels, and comic books in the franchise, there's also a a movie in the works from New Line Cinema.

Cliff serves as Epic Games' design director and he's a 17-year veteran of the computer and video game industry. In fact, Cliff shipped his first commercial game, *Jazz Jackrabbit*, before graduating from high school. He continues to lend his creative expertise to Epic's upcoming projects such as *Shadow Complex*, which is based on bestselling author Orson Scott Card's latest novel, *Empire*. Cliff has expanded the scope of his work to include other entertainment sectors as well.

With iconic artistic qualities and an epic story line, *Gears of War* was ingeniously designed by Cliff from the ground up to be spun into movies, graphic novels, and the like.

"The first game I ever played was *Space Invaders* on the Atari 2600," says Cliff. "I was instantly hooked by the idea of manipulating images on my television screen but wasn't quite old enough or aware that this could be a possible career. The title that inspired me the most would have to be the original *Super Mario Bros* on the Nintendo Entertainment System. There was something about these cartoony worlds that unfolded before me that were filled with secrets that, at the time, I believed were not meant to be discovered by the designers."

When he was a kid, Cliff liked to play any and all games that he could get his hands on, including old Nintendo games like *Deadly Towers* and *Athena*. What he didn't

realize at the time was that this was his training for his job today. He
eventually got an Apple IIc and Basic and started cranking
out Infocom-style text adventure games. He then graduated to an
IBM 386 SX and a copy of Visual Basic that he used to start making
graphical adventures similar to *Déjà Vu* and *Uninvited*.

"I sold copies of my games out of my mother's house in Ziploc
bags around when the CompuServe forums and the shareware
industry were in full swing," says Cliff. "I checked out a little game
called *Jill of the Jungle* that had a call for talented partners at the
end of it. I sent a prototype of my next adventure over to Tim
Sweeney and Mark Rein, and within days Mark called me to gush
about how cool my game was, and he pitched all sorts of ideas for
improvements, which terrified my then seventeen-year-old self.
Luckily, he didn't scare me away. I later partnered with them to
build *Jazz Jackrabbit* and eventually went on to *Unreal* and
Unreal Tournament."

As Epic's design director, Cliff contributes to the creative

process for all of the company's games and related media. He spends a lot of time developing the *Gears of War* universe by figuring out what new elements to add while staying true to the series, testing new content for *Gears of War 2*, and also working on secret, unannounced projects.

"Games generally start out as high-level concepts," explains Cliff. "Once a team drafts the initial design treatment, the game moves into preproduction and prototyping. At Epic, we use tools like Unreal Kismet to mock up potential enemies and weapons, for example. Once you start building out the world, you have to figure out the core game-play loop, which is the basic idea behind the game that makes it fun. During production, you also have to decide what features are essential to making your game fun, cut nonessential 'like-to-have' items, and polish, polish, polish. Iteration and great user feedback is key to making a good game."

Epic Games also creates the technology, called Unreal Engine

fast fact

Because it was built on the Unreal 3 game engine, *Gears of War* required only 20–30 people working on it full-time. This base code allowed the design team to focus on how to make the game cooler than ever without having to build a new engine from scratch.

3, that powers games such as Sony Online Entertainment's *DC Universe Online* and 2K Games' *Bioshock 2.* "A game engine is a complex piece of software on top of which you build your game, and it ties together key systems like rendering, physics, animation, audio, networking code, artificial intelligence," Cliff explains. Epic continually makes improvements to the Unreal Engine and is a big supporter of game developers everywhere.

Cliff says that for a career in video games, playing games is important, although he likes to think that a variety of life experiences and cultural references are the best grist for the mill. Inspiration can come from so many places—random dreams, graphic novels, socializing with friends, amazing road trips—that you never know when or where a cool idea will surface. He thinks it's important to surround yourself with as many pop culture and literary influences as possible, because that will ultimately make you a better game designer.

"Getting into games takes a lot of hard work, a lot of talent,

> ❝ I was instantly hooked by the idea of manipulating images on my television screen. . . . The title that inspired me the most would have to be the original Super Mario Bros. ❞

No game happens without inspiration, and Cliff credits the games that helped spark him to create the spectacular *Gears of War: Kill Switch. Resident Evil 4* helped inform the design and game play of the series, while *Bionic Commando* influenced the movement and motion.

and also a bit of luck," Cliff says. "If you're more of an artist you should acquire as much traditional training as you can and then move on to creating digital works. If you're more math and problem-solving oriented you should look into learning various programming languages."

He continues, "Ultimately, succeeding in games will require a lot of trial and error. You have to be willing to throw away the first thousand images you create. Your portfolio is only as strong as your weakest

link. You need to network online and eventually get to the Game Developers Conference, show up with copies of your work, and get feedback from professionals firsthand." Cliff thinks the games industry is very accessible and most industry pros are friendly. "If you are a hard worker with talent, you will catch their attention. You just have to make sure your work and ideas get into the right hands. You can do that by posting your samples online or attending special gaming conferences in your area," he says.

"Mod making [creating new levels or variations on an existing game] is another great way to get started in the business," adds Cliff. "A significant number of Epic employees got started in the mod community, and now they're living the dream of making triple-A [blockbuster] titles." ■

Art Simulates Life

Will Wright
creator, stupid fun club
the Sims; Spore

Job Skills Needed: Computers; Creativity

Will first became a big name in gaming when he developed *SimCity*, the acclaimed, nonviolent, open-ended simulation game. Will followed up the success of *SimCity* with a string of popular simulation games throughout the 1990s. Titles such as *SimEarth: The Living Planet* (1990), *SimAnt: The Electronic Ant Colony* (1991), *SimCity 2000* (1993), *SimCopter* (1996), and *SimCity 3000* (1999) introduced simulation games to hundreds of thousands of new fans, demonstrating the genre's potential.

Will's next groundbreaking game was *The Sims* (2000), which has gone on to become the bestselling PC game franchise of all time and is now available in 22 languages in 60 countries. Will, who studied architecture in college, originally created the software to help architects design buildings. To "score" the quality of the

With a string of hit titles including *The Sims* and now *Spore,* Will uses his platform as a successful game designer to encourage aspiring designers to let their minds wander and take risks with their concepts.

design, he added tiny people who would inhabit the buildings. These simulated people quickly stole the spotlight, and Will realized that watching the lives of these Sims unfold was the real entertainment. *The Sims* franchise has gone on to sell more than 100 million units worldwide.

Widely acknowledged for creating the simulation genre, Will unveiled *Spore* in 2008. *Spore* allows players to create a species, help it build a society, develop its culture, and explore an infinite cosmos of worlds created by other players. *Spore* has been distinguished with such honors as *Popular Science*'s Best of What's New Award, *Popular Mechanics*' Breakthrough

Award, *PC Magazine*'s Technical Excellence Award, and the Jim Henson Technology Honor. *Rolling Stone* named Will one of the 100 People Who Are Changing America in March 2009, which placed him among artists, leaders, scientists, and policy makers who are "fighting every day to show us what is possible."

Will credits his passion for models as a kid for getting him into games. "I always liked games as a kid, and I always liked making models," Will recalls. "And my model making slowly evolved into building robots—things with motors that would drive around. I bought my first computer to control my robots and ended up teaching myself to program, and in doing that I started learning about things like artificial intelligence and simulation and started realizing that I could build little simulations on the computer."

In many ways, that idea of creating an environment in a game continues today. "The best examples of those worlds, at the time and even now, are games where the players are making these little

simulated worlds, which, in some sense, is a form of modeling."

Will considers this combination of passion and practical experience a key to his success. "When I would build models, I would always build models of things that interested me. I was very interested in military history and aviation and space life and things like that. And in building a model, I found that I was just kind of naturally learning more about these subjects. And so, on the computer, the same thing happens. When I build a model of the way a city works, I end up researching a lot about cities and their dynamics and behavior. And so modeling, for me, is a great way to learn about something."

But his interests also helped him understand the importance of learning the fundamentals taught in school, now that he had found his ideal outlet to apply them. "For me, I was okay in math. I never really enjoyed it that much. But I'm into building these model worlds, and at some point math became a tool for me.

When I realized what I could do with math, it all suddenly became fascinating. It was totally a matter of how relevant it was to what I wanted to do," he says.

In addition to finding ways to build off the basics he learned in class, Will also feels the school of hard knocks was an important part of his learning process. "I see the entire path I've taken as a learning experience, and I'm not sure I could really short-circuit that and take something that I had learned years later and bring it [back] in time. I don't think it would have had that much meaning for me at that point. I probably would not have listened to myself from the future."

As in a linear role-playing game (RPG), where the hero has to perform specific tasks in sequence to advance, Will still considers himself a student. "I had to slowly build up my experience. So just the process of me going through my career and doing things I've done, I've learned probably more from my failures than I

have my successes. One of the things I would definitely not want to do is go back in time and tell myself, 'Don't do this. It's gonna fail,' because I would've basically avoided a very deep learning experience."

Will thinks that "the most important skill, by far, and, in fact, it's more than a skill" is "to develop an appreciation for how fun learning can be." He says, "A lot of times, people, especially kids, associate learning with sitting in school for hours on end and being bored. But most of the effective learning that I've had in my lifetime was stuff that I wanted to learn, and I went out and learned on my own.

"Teachers can help you and guide you and give you background and maybe even introduce you to things that you normally wouldn't trip across, but I think from a kid or adult's point of view, I think the primary thing that I've come away with is that you need

❝ One of the things I would definitely not want to do is go back in time and tell myself, 'Don't do this. It's gonna fail,' because I would've basically avoided a very deep learning experience. **❞**

Will believes that learning and being creative is a lifetime process, and that there is no substitute for getting out in the world and expanding one's horizons.

to take responsibility for your own education. Don't just sit in class for eight hours a day assuming you're going to automatically find something that motivates or inspires you."

Will concludes, "I think the best advice is to find something you love doing, and if you love doing it, you'll do well, and if you don't really enjoy what you're doing, you're not going to do it as well, no matter how hard you try." ∎

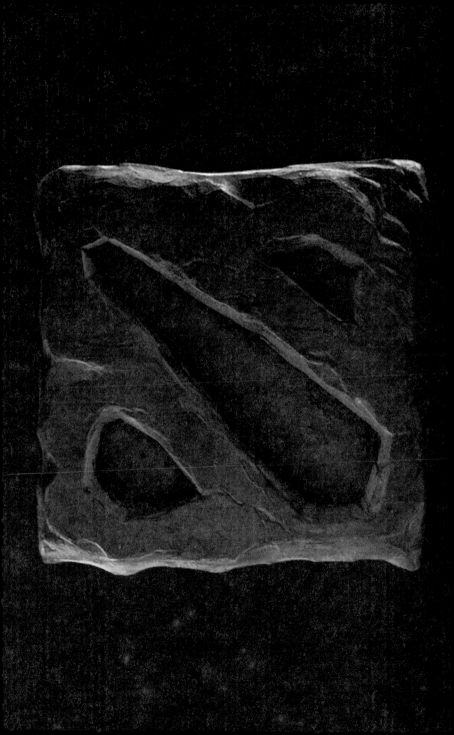

calling the game

Troels 'syndereN' Nielsen
professional video game competition commentator,
organizer, coach, and player *Dota 2*

Job Skills Needed: Critical Analysis; Game Knowledge;
Enthusiasm; Personality; a Good Voice

omething very interesting happened when people flipped
the television to famous sports channels ESPN 2 and ESPN
3 in July 2014. Typically, viewers can expect these channels
to show a few baseball highlights or preseason NFL talk this time
of year, but this summer, something quite different greeted
sports fans watching ESPN: Video gaming.

In particular, they saw one video game called *Dota 2*, which
was smack in the middle of staging the biggest, most important
video-game competition to that point in history, and as such, was
broadcasting on the same channel where the World Cup had
been seen just a few days before. Including the ESPN viewers and
those who took in the dozens of epic gaming battles online, 20

million people watched 19 teams slug it out that July in an epic tournament called The International 2014, which raged for over a week to find out who was the very best at *Dota 2*.

The game, for those unfamiliar, pits two teams of five players (no more, no less) against each other on a standardized map where they control unique units called "heroes" in a battle of deep strategy, with the goal to kill the other team and, eventually, destroy their base and win the match. *Dota 2* is breakneck-paced, thoroughly complex, and, above all, absolutely thrilling even at amateur levels—and with the undisputed best players in the world involved, The International 2014 was a spectacle on par with any of the more traditional sporting world championships that had come and gone in the months before.

Though *Dota 2* gameplay is thrilling in itself, a large part of the gripping energy and brilliant entertainment that The International brought to viewers worldwide was owed to

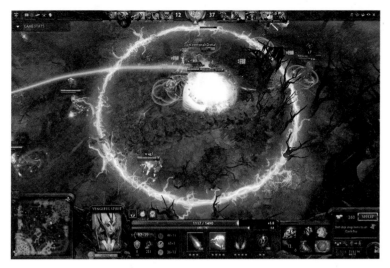

Announcing a game of pro *Dota 2* is no mean feat. There are 107 distinct characters available in *Dota 2*, each of which has its own unique moves and strategies, and each of which pairs very differently with each other character. Commentators must intimately know all characters and how they work together so that they can relay that info to the audience.

something other than the action on the map. What really pushed The International over the top and more than earned its spot on ESPN was the top-notch presentation of the competition by a team of event organizers and broadcasters, who brought a level of professionalism and quality to the live streaming of The International that is more often associated with other major league sports championships.

There were producers, dozens of cameramen, an enormous venue complete with a stage decked out in brilliant lights, huge LED screens and speakers, and a team of expert commentators and analysts that guided the viewer through each and every match with talk that was both enlightening and entertaining.

This cadre of ESPN and online commentators was made up of former and current pro *Dota 2* players, game statisticians and analysts. Among them was one Troels "syndereN" Nielsen, a 24-year-old from Denmark who retired from professional *Dota* play in December 2013 and moved into full-time event work, which included coaching players, organizing competitions, and, most famously, commentating or "casting" pro *Dota 2* games.

Nielsen's job titles didn't even exist a few years ago. Casting, especially, is a very new field of work that is coming into its own, with a small number of talented youngsters like Nielsen leading the charge. When asked to summarize what it is he does in these very new types of jobs, Nielsen told us the following:

"As a tournament organizer, I contact and keep track of different teams and make sure to set up matches and times to keep a tournament running in a stable way. As a private coach, I teach one or multiple people at once different things about the

syndereN has been a fixture at some of the world's biggest video game tournaments, including the one with the biggest money prize ever, the 2014 Dota 2 International.

game that they are interested in learning—much as a school teacher—just in a computer game. As a color commentator, my job is to add detail to the commentary. This means that my main job is to explain strategy and decisions players make, while it is mainly the play-by-play commentator who narrates the fights and what is going on on the screen right now."

Since competitive gaming, or eSports, has not existed in the world for very long, Nielsen did not initially set out to become an online commentator; his role came as a natural evolution of his passion for video games and his talent at mastering and explaining them. Nielsen gamed for fun through high school, saying his "first gaming job, and actually the majority of my gaming so far, took place while I attended high school and

The whole point of a *Dota* match is, in the end, to do what you see here and destroy the other team's "ancient," but getting to this point in a professional game takes a level of knowledge, skill, and dedication that is on par with any other competitive activity.

university. I found a good balance between playing on a high level without sacrificing my studies."

After graduating from Aalborg University in summer 2013, Nielsen decided to kick things up a notch, and his focus helped him to find a place in the pro-gaming circuit. "Gaming was always a big hobby for me," he told us, "and I just really liked playing games. I tried to get better all the time, and at some point, I was good enough to get offered to play for a competitive team. It was amazing for me that I got the opportunity to turn my biggest hobby into something professional!" Nielsen's shot at pro-gaming went very well. "Since then," he said, "I've been focused fully on eSports."

That focus served Nielsen quite well indeed in his efforts,

Dota is intensely detailed and stats-based, and it often turns out that the players that have the most expansive know-how of the game's mathematical core end up the victors.

and he was soon rewarded with a huge win at the important DreamHack Winter *Dota* competition in 2011. After continued success with a variety of teams, Nielsen took the opportunity to move to the analyst side of competitive gaming, something he was able to do due to his extensive experience on the pro circuit: "Having played professionally before, I know the situations in the game, the strategy, and the thought the players have while playing, and therefore understand the game better than most others," he said.

It turned out to be the perfect time to make the jump to commentating. As competitive gaming exploded in popularity, Nielsen's skills as a player and commentator led to big opportunities in the world of game competitions. He told us, "As

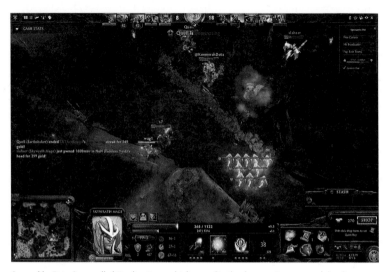

Games like Dota 2 are called "mobas," or multiplayer online battle arena" games, and they have grown in popularity with impressive quickness since their beginning in the early 2000s.

a caster, I suppose my biggest breaks were commentating at The International 2 and 4, the largest *Dota 2* event of the year with millions of dollars on the line and millions watching worldwide."

After the immense success of the International 4 in July 2014, things are only going to get bigger and better for gaming, eSports, *Dota*, and Nielsen. Competitive gaming is growing and creating new opportunities, he said. "I've really enjoyed it so far. Having your hobby as your job is a dream."

With the industry expanding so rapidly, and its popularity as an entertainment form growing every day, opportunities in casting, coaching, and analyzing online games will also grow over the next few years. This is essentially creating a new segment within the video gaming industry, one that focuses primarily on the gameplay itself, instead of creating or reviewing games. For

those looking to get into the industry, Nielsen said this:

"Make sure you enjoy what you do. If you love telling stories, love using your voice and getting people excited over something, commentating might be something for you to pursue as a career. Make sure you can handle criticism and be critical of your own work so you can improve. As with everything else, it requires a lot of work, but if gaming is your hobby, you will likely not get as exhausted with it as you would with a lot of other work. I guess three key words for a good commentator are enthusiasm, personality, and, obviously, a good voice. People need to want to listen to you!"

From the success he's seen in the burgeoning eSports industry, it's clear that plenty of folks out there do indeed want to listen to Nielsen, and it may just be that he'll go down as a pioneer in a whole new form of mainstream entertainment. ■

paid to play

Johnathan "Fatal1ty" Wendel
professional video gamer

Job Skills Needed: Hand-eye coordination; Reflexes; Determination

Ever wish you could play video games for a living? Today there's actually a career for professional gamers, thanks to global video game leagues like Major League Gaming. One of the first professional gamers to rise through the ranks in America was Johnathan, best known as "Fatal1ty" to opponents and fans alike. Wendel has won 12 world titles in five different games and is the most recognizable face in eSports which is the one I see most these day. In 2007, he was presented with the first Lifetime Achievement Award in the history of pro gaming.

Back in 1999, Johnathan became the first professional gamer in the United States. After winning $4,000 in his first PC gaming tournament in Dallas, Texas, Johnathan traveled from tournament to competition around the globe full-time, playing id Software's

Johnathan has won more than $500,000 playing in video game tournaments over the years, including a $150,000 check for winning a world championship.

Though formal eSports events have grown in popularity over the years, competing for money through games is no new concept: The idea dates back to some of the first titles ever released in arcades.

Quake for cash and prizes. He traversed five continents in his first year as a pro, racking up wins all along the way.

"No one was really making a living playing video games," says Johnathan. "There was some money to be won, just not full-time money. It eventually picked up to where it became a definite possibility, so I took advantage of the situation and ended up winning over $100,000 my first year as a pro."

Johnathan played sports throughout

school and did pretty well in traditional classes while excelling at math. All during high school, he gamed on the side and competed in small tournaments.

"When I graduated from high school, I realized there were tournaments offering big money for the game I was super passionate about," explains Johnathan. "One of the guys I trained with won a big tourney in Europe, so that's when I realized I had the talent to win. I competed from then through today, and even started a great business making products for gamers around the world, working with Creative, XFX, and OCZ. So now I work pretty hard with the companies that develop new Fatal1ty Brand products, everything from headphones, power supplies, graphic cards, and sound cards."

Johnathan has won more than $500,000 playing in video game tournaments over the years, including a $150,000 check for taking home the top prize in the 2005 CPL World Championship. Today he spends a lot of his time running Fatal1ty Inc., which makes new video game products to help

other gamers become better at competitions.

"I realized I needed different equipment than what was being offered to step up my game to the next level, so I decided to start designing and making my own products," says Johnathan. "Eventually, it turned into a very successful business that helps gamers all around the world play at the highest level."

Gaming remains a big part of Johnathan's life. He spends four to eight hours a day playing games. He loves the experience and the competition of playing the best players around the world from the comfort of his own home. He says that like American gamers, the Europeans are great competitors, especially gamers from countries like Sweden and Finland.

"Obviously, console gaming has done well and more people are getting into gaming through Wii, but to be on the cutting edge of gaming, the PC is always the first one to have anything," says Johnathan. "Look at *World of Warcraft*. It's one of the most popular games in the world, and it's only available on the PC.

I'm also a big fan of the Xbox 360 and Nintendo Wii, but when
it comes to playing first-person shooters or being more enticed to
my game where I want to do something different, I love the PC
for that. The quality of graphics and sound are ten times better
than the console."

Although he took an unconventional path, Johnathan says
there are a million ways to get into the gaming business, from
programming to art to marketing and every other possibility.

"Just find out what you would love to do, and in gaming
you'll most likely find that job," said Johnathan. "Kids today are
more hardwired than ever before. I was lucky to see computers
still booming, so I know exactly how a PC works and how all the
code affects the program or game. I feel young kids today,
though, have a huge advantage in technology over the generation
I grew up with."

When he's not working or practicing, Johnathan likes to keep
competitive, playing real sports and card games. ■

Imagining Mayhem

Joshua Ortega
Game scriptwriter

Joshua's work spans nearly the entire spectrum of the popular arts. He has written for every major American comic book company, including Marvel, DC Comics, Dark Horse, Image, and more, working on high-profile properties such as *Star Wars*, *Spider-Man*, *Star Trek*, *Frank Frazetta's Death Dealer*, and *Battlestar Galactica*.

A former journalist, Joshua is also the author of a wide variety of Xbox 360 titles for Microsoft Game Studios, including the bestselling smash hit *Gears of War 2*. He has been featured numerous times on National Public Radio and has also appeared on the Sci Fi Channel, FOX TV, G4, and XPlay, in addition to many other major media outlets.

He was drawn to video games by his fascination with the

" " This industry is changing the world, and I'm very proud to be a part of it. As we joke sometimes, 'Look, Ma, playing all of those games did pay off!' **" "**

As graphics improve and characters look more realistic all the time, it is critical for the scriptwriters to ensure that the story and depth behind each character evolve as well.

interactive screen. "Video games, interactive entertainment, dynamic storytelling, whatever term we use to describe this medium, I'm just really excited that we're finally being recognized as a legitimate art form," he said. "I think we, as gamers, have always known this on an intuitive level. But now we're the major art form, we're pushing the boundaries of storytelling and art, of design and technology, and it's just a fantastic place

❝❝ When everyone is synced up and working together, you can put out an amazing piece of art and an amazing product that satisfies the needs of the publisher, (the) developer, and the people who play. **❞❞**

to be. This industry is changing the world, and I'm very proud to be a part of it. As we joke sometimes, 'Look, Ma, playing all of those games *did* pay off!'"

Joshua took a typically atypical path to the industry, attending college but not graduating. Instead, he focused on honing his skills and pursuing his passion, which he admits may not be the best route for everyone.

His first big break in the industry came when his novel ((*Frequencies*)), comics, and graphic novels gained notoriety. "That really paved the way for my work in the games industry. By proving myself in other media, it allowed me to work on

No longer can a game succeed with bland, generic characters—even if they look really cool. Games need good storytellers to add insight and emotion to the splashiest of graphics and most excessive of explosions.

A big challenge of writing for a game can be working on sequels. When working on a story someone else started, writers must make sure the new story line faithfully carries on the legacy of the original while providing sensible new depth and detail.

triple-A titles like *Gears of War 2*, *Blue Dragon*, and *Lost Odyssey*.

"If we're talking about specifics, then I'd say my big break was writing the 'bridge' story that connected the *Knights of the Old Republic* for Dark Horse Comics, Lucasfilm, and Bioware. That story really proved to people that I knew games, loved the medium, and was willing to do the research necessary to respect the franchise, continuity, and, most importantly for me, the story."

Joshua believes his ability to fulfill his role as a storyteller, and to be a team player, are the keys to his success. To do his job well, he says a writer needs to

"make sure that he is always synchronized with the developer and designers, is intimately involved with the early stages of level design, and is also collaborating with the other essential parts of the team. When everyone is synced up and working together, you can put out an amazing piece of art and an amazing product that satisfies the needs of the publisher, [the] developer, and the people who play."

He thinks kids should not be afraid to follow their dreams. "It can sound clichéd," he says, "but it's the most important thing you can do in your life. Be prepared for hard work and dedication, and also be prepared for those who will tell you [you] cannot succeed. Don't let them get in your way; they're roadblocks on your life's journey, and you need to steer around them. Only by doing what you love will you truly be able to succeed." ■

Writing For Fun & Games

Journalists' Faceoff

We gathered two veteran writers and editors from the world of video games to discuss their corner of the industry and explore how they got where they are. While outsiders may think writing about video games is all fun and games, it's not. With us today are Dean Takahashi, blogger for VentureBeat.com; and Joe Funk, owner and editor at Mojo-Media.com.

First question is obvious: How did you get started?

Dean: I became a journalist first. I always loved reading, writing, and gaming. I majored in English at the University of California at Berkeley, but even in college I spent too many quarters and too much time in the arcades. I learned firsthand about journalism while working at the Institute for Journalism Education at Berkeley, and then went on to get a master's degree in journalism at Northwestern University. I started work and spent many hours playing games in my free time. But this avocation didn't combine with my vocation for many years. I migrated to covering tech news at the San Jose Mercury News in 1994 and have covered tech news in Silicon Valley ever since. In 1996, I started a job in the San Francisco bureau of the Wall Street Journal. I was the youngest guy in the office and I inherited the video game beat. I wrote stories where the primary aim was to explain to nongamer adults what their kids were doing. At that point, I began to cover the video game business continually for other outlets and wrote two books on the making of Microsoft's Xbox business. In 2008, I joined VentureBeat, a tech news blog.

Joe: I was hooked the moment I played the first Atari Pong console when I was seven years old, mesmerized by the concept of interacting with the images on my TV screen instead of just passively watching them, even if it was just a one-color blip of light at that time. This led to a lifetime of embracing technology and finding ways to develop my passion into a career. I majored in contemporary American history in college and served as editor of the student newspaper for three years. I began working at the magazine Electronic Gaming Monthly in 1991 and worked my way up from entry-level assistant editor to become editorial director of the entire group, responsible for five monthly magazines and several one-shot publications. Ziff-Davis acquired us in 1997 and I remained editorial director of the Ziff-Davis Game Group where, among other stuff, I was a cofounder of the Official U.S. PlayStation Magazine and VideoGames.com. After nine years, I left ZD in 2000 and founded Mojo Media, where we have since become a leading supplier and packager of editorial and advertorial content for video games, sports, and other enthusiast interests for websites, magazines, and books. I wrote two books on the history of Electronic Arts and Madden NFL Football, and have been part of several New York Times nonfiction bestsellers.

so, is it really all just fun and games?

Joe: Ha! Well, in a way, yes! But there is always a trade-off when you turn a passion into your profession. It can become easy to get too absorbed in your job and the environment because your passion is real, while the rest of your life is whizzing by. I'll always love interactive entertainment, but as I get older I have fewer big blocks of uninterrupted time for gaming, so I find myself playing more tablet based games because they are portable and it is easier to jump in and out of the action.

Dean: I don't review games on a regular basis. Rather, I review games occasionally. But I write about the business of video games almost every day. It's not easy, because the video game business has become a worldwide industry with many different pieces. The tentacles range from iPhone games to hardcore console games to free web games. All of it is constantly changing. I don't get to spend as much time as I'd like playing games and relaxing. Often, I find that I have to play games that I ordinarily wouldn't choose myself, for the sake of understanding a new part of the business. It's hard work and comes with a lot of challenges.

what classes or extracurricular activities at school helped prepare you for this job?

Dean: I took one computer science class, but that is outdated and it never proved useful to me. I think it was really important that I learned how to be a journalist, which involves collecting facts and writing fast. That's the backbone of my job as a video game business writer. But I also have to play games to understand and write about them.

Joe: Working for my college newspaper provided the most practical experience and had a big influence on my career path. I was also fortunate enough to have a few great teachers and mentors along my way to earning a B.A. in history. That, combined with a passion for playing video games, helped inform my decision to try and somehow get a job in the video games industry even if it meant starting at the bottom.

Any advice for kids thinking about starting out today?

Dean: I believe that youngsters should practice writing their own reviews and publishing them on their own blogs. There are fewer obstacles than ever to publishing your work, so take advantage of that. Focus on continuous improvement, read the columns of people you admire, and decipher how they put those columns together. Repeat that over and over. Eventually, you can show your blog posts to potential employers and get freelance or part-time writing gigs. You should also find ways to seek out classes on journalism or writing, and pursue internships with websites or newspapers. You can be an opinionated reviewer, but you'll set yourself apart from the crowd if you're a talented journalist.

Joe: It's all good to think big, but don't expect to be a home-run hitter right off the bat. Hitting singles and doubles and taking small steps at the outset of your career is fine, so be committed, stay focused, and be prepared to grind, grind, grind. The industry will continue to expand and specialize, so whether you end up working on, or writing about, iOS games, blockbuster console titles like Gears of War, Minecraft, or space simulations for NASA, there will be more opportunities in the future than there are today, so try a lot of different stuff, figure out what you really like, and start reaching for it now!

Job Glossary

There is a wide variety of creative jobs requiring different skill sets in the video games industry. From music to motion capture, from alpha to beta testing, there are many different jobs and careers you can begin preparing for now. While the constant march of technology means that roles are always evolving and sometimes the line between jobs becomes blurred, the occupations listed below include many of the traditional gigs you will encounter in the industry.

Marc Mencher, a top game industry talent agent and president of GamerRecruiter.com, said "Our industry has been in a hiring war for several years...I have a lot of jobs to fill! Some really optimistic predictions claim that software design jobs will grow by 54.6 percent and publishing jobs will grow by 67.9 percent in several years. The demand for tech workers right now is so great that game companies routinely compete with Goliaths such as Google and Amazon, who need workers with the same skills."

2-D Conceptual Artist

Among the few artists in video game production who create physical pieces of art, 2-D concept artists are especially important in the early stages of a game. They draw out characters and scenes for the other artists to base their designs on, storyboard video cut scenes, and sometimes even create load screens and manual art.

2-D Texture Artist

Even as games become more and more 3-D oriented, the 2-D texture artist retains an important position in the art design of a game. Creating the walls, textures, landscapes, and even faces of characters, 2-D texture artists are responsible for a great deal of a title's realism.

3-D Character Animator

Once the game characters have been designed, it's time to make sure they move the way they are supposed to: People need to walk and run realistically, animals need to have the proper gait, and machines need to move robotically. It's up to the 3-D character animators to create realistic movements, either by hand or by using motion capture technology.

3-D Character Builder

Starting with a piece of concept art or a character from a licensed story, the 3-D character builders are responsible for designing the different animals, machines, people, and creatures in a game. Working closely with the other artists and the programming staff, it's their job to turn epic heroes and villains into moving beings.

3-D Cut Scene Artist

This is a perfect field for an artist with a background or interest in animation and film production, as 3-D cut scene artists work from storyboards to create the video cut scenes in a game. With lighting, production, voice, music, and many other variables to focus on, these artists work as a team to make movie-quality scenes within the game.

3-D Model Builder (Objects)

Object specialists have very rewarding and very focused jobs—designing the objects within a game, from weapons to furniture to vehicles and even buildings. They must be goal oriented, knowing when an object has just the right amount of detail for the game it is in while also understanding the real-life intricacies of the object they've built.

Art Director

To become an art director, an artist needs to know just about everything there is about game-production, from 3-D mapping to character design. Art directors oversee the art staff, making sure the right people are in the right jobs and keeping everything coordinated. Troubleshooting problems and keeping artists focused is a big responsibility, and it's up to the art director to make sure everything goes smoothly.

Art Technician

All-purpose troubleshooters as well as important for keeping a design team up to date on the latest technologies, art technicians need to have boundless energy and an eye for efficiency. As they are commonly responsible for purchasing and maintaining the hardware and software the art team uses, art technicians need to be on the cutting edge of technology.

Associate Producer

The tasks of the associate producer (AP) change depending on the game he or she is working on and who the producer is, but the basic role of the job is one of support. APs help the producer manage the project while also filtering ideas from staff and the public. Normally an AP is focused on interfacing with the testing department and localizing the game for foreign markets.

Audio Programmer and Engineer

As games become bigger and more detailed and require more dynamic sounds, the jobs of audio programmers and engineers have become bigger and bigger. They work with the composer and writers to figure out how to synthesize sounds and music as well as implement them within the game, and their responsibilities can range from the smallest of noises to the thematic crescendos of a game climax.

Composer / Sound Engineer or Designer

Every game needs to have its backing soundtrack, and the composer is the person who gives a title its score. Whether it is sweeping classical strings for a dramatic moment or pulsing techno-pop to get the blood moving, every game needs to have the right musical accompaniment. Composers work much like film composers, selecting music to put in the game or writing the music themselves. Plus, think of all the sounds that go into a game that aren't music. There can be footsteps, voices, explosions, swords clashing, leaves rustling, and thousands of other details that go into a game's audio. Sound engineers and designers are responsible for bringing these sounds to life within the game, working with programmers to give every moment its sound.

Engine / Tools Programmer

The engine of a game is like its brain. Engine and tools programmers have very important roles in the production of video games. First, they are responsible for the code base that a game is built on, making it imperative that they be expert programmers. They also must have an understanding of the roles of other programmers, artists, and even level designers working on a project, since they create easy-to-use tools for nontechnical folks who need to be able to use the engine to make the rest of the game.

Executive Producer / Producer

Filling one of the toughest and most rewarding jobs in video games, producers have to wear several different hats at once. They are in charge of keeping a game on task, budgeting, and scheduling the project while making sure that the team members are kept happy and working efficiently. Producers represent the game and the people who work on it, putting in long hours to make sure the project is done the right way.

Game Designer / Lead Designer

Game designers work with just about every member of a game project. Designers collaborate with testers and programmers to make sure every game is all it can be, organizing all of the different elements to follow an overall plan for the game. The designer of a game is both a visionary and an effective team leader. It is important to make sure the people on the design team are working toward the same goal; the lead designer coordinates their efforts and takes on the role of decision maker along with the producer.

Game Writer

Just like their counterparts in Hollywood, game writers are in charge of scripting the scenes of a game. They write the story within the game, adding dialogue and on-screen text to bring a game idea to life. Their work can be as wide-ranging as a novel-length story with multiple scenarios for an RPG, a play-by-play for a sports game, or a linear story for an action or adventure game.

Graphics / Special Effects Programmer

While all game programmers have to understand graphics to do their jobs, it is the job of the graphics programmer to be an expert in this domain. Bringing 3-D realism to a 2-D screen is no easy task, so the graphics programmer must be goal oriented and focused, with an artistic mind-set.

Junior Programmer

This is the perfect entry-level position for a person with programming skills and a passion for video games. Junior programmers are the people who start to bring a game concept to life. Starting with a basic understanding of programming, they are trained in specific areas such as 3-D rendering and animation, artificial intelligence (AI) development, and physics.

Lead Programmer

The head of the programming team, the lead programmer is responsible for complicated coding and decision making as well as networking with other aspects of game production, especially the writing team. Responsible for making sure all of the code from different programmers works as a single unit, the lead programmer takes many parts to make a whole.

Lead Quality Assurance Tester

The lead tester is the person in charge of assembling and managing the testing team. Working closely with the production and design teams, the lead tester creates the testing schedule and maps out what exactly needs to be tested with each version of the game. This is a technical job requiring the ability to cut code and program like a junior programmer. The testing department actually works hand in hand with the programming department to make sure the code created is stable and functional.

Level Builder

Working with the level designers, programmers, writers, and testers, the level builder has to tie many different elements together to create a cohesive world or level within a game. Stitching everything together makes the game flow the way it should, and level builders help place objects, enemies, checkpoints, and other elements in their proper places.

Level Designer

Level designers are responsible for the underpinnings of specific levels or areas of a game, and focus their efforts on the game play for portions of the project. Level designers place enemies, obstacles, puzzles, and checkpoints within their areas of expertise, providing goals and challenges for players.

Marketing and Public Relations

The marketing and public relations staffs have important jobs in the production of a game, making sure the word gets out about the title in development. They keep fans and the media saturated with screen shots and updates about the game's progress, then tout the features and greatness of the title as it nears its release.

multiplayer networking programmer

As the demand for multiplayer online games has increased, so, too, has the demand for programmers to work on multiplayer networks. In addition to understanding the game and what players want, these programmers need to work with the limitations of their engines as well as the systems they are working on, while also being wary of security holes that may allow cheating or hackers.

playability game tester

One of the most fun but demanding jobs in the world of video games is that of the game tester. Patience is the key virtue of testers: Their job is to play the game over and over—and over again. Sometimes they just run along a wall in a game, or one level, looking to isolate bugs and document them so the design team can fix them.

project manager

Similar to a producer, a project manager is more focused on business operations issues such as meeting budgets and milestone objectives so the game company is profitable. Assigning tasks and managing time are the key roles of the project manager. Often a project manager is teamed with a producer. The producer focuses on production issues, and the project manager focuses on following up with every person working on a game to make sure all departments are on task and ready to finish their assignments on time and within budget.

sales

The sales staff is responsible for the end result of all the design team's hard work: people buying the game they've put their hearts and souls into creating. Working with retail outlets, websites, and other distributors, salespeople help get the game in the store and then into gamers' hands. They help place displays in stores and keep the hype in motion after a game is released.